A DADDY LONGLEGS
Isn't a Spider

by Melissa Stewart
Illustrated by John Himmelman

Windward Publishing
Lakeville, Minnesota

ISBN: 978-0-89317-069-1

Windward Publishing
An Imprint of Finney Company
8075 215th Street West
Lakeville, Minnesota 55044
www.finneyco.com

ECO-FRIENDLY BOOKS
Made in the USA

1 3 5 7 9 10 8 6 4 2
Printed in the United States of America in Stevens Point, Wisconsin.
    091509
    09, 102643

Special thanks to Rod Crawford, Curator of Arachnids,
Thomas Burke Memorial Washington State Museum,
University of Washington, for his suggestions and advice.

For Colin, Claire, and Caroline—M.S.
For Lipsy-lou—J.H.

On a warm spring day, a tiny daddy longlegs bursts out of her egg. She is no larger than the head of a pin. Her body is pure white and her eyes are as black as coal.

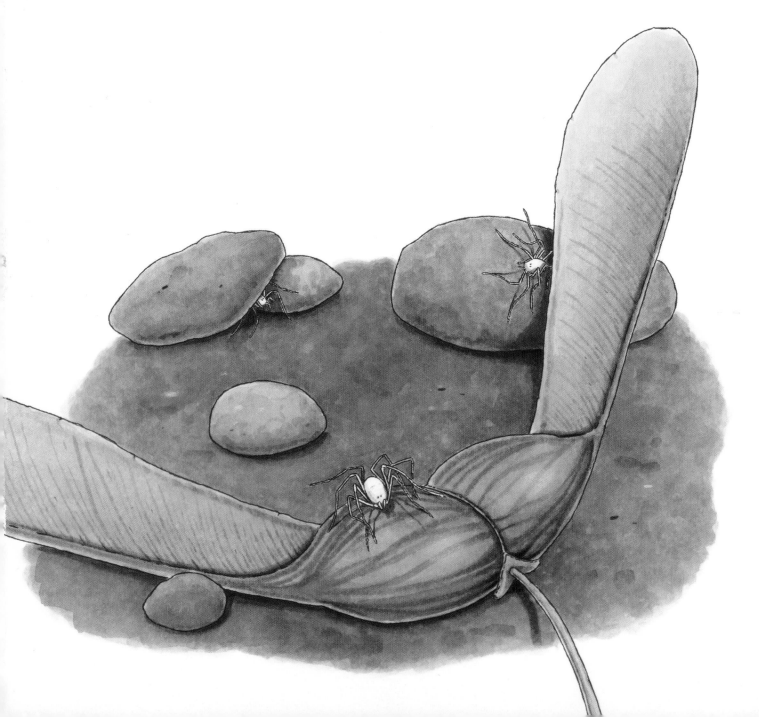

The daddy longlegs grows so quickly that she needs to shed her tough outer covering before she's even an hour old. As soon as her exoskeleton splits open, she climbs out of her old skin. Then she uses her sharp jaws to free her long, slender legs.

The daddy longlegs continues to grow quickly. Over the next few weeks, she sheds her exo-skeleton six more times.

During the final molt, one of her long legs accidentally breaks off. But even with seven legs, she can still move fast enough to catch aphids.

All through the summer,
the daddy longlegs spends her
days resting in a cool, moist
place. She is well hidden from
hornets and other enemies.

In the late afternoon, pale bands of pink and orange clouds streak across the darkening western sky. Long friendly shadows slowly creep across the old stone wall. The daddy longlegs shakes herself awake and scurries to the ground.

As she heads out to hunt, she passes a marbled spider perched on its web. But the two arachnids don't notice each other. The daddy longlegs looks similar to the spider. For example, both have eight legs. But there are some important differences.

Spider
- Two body parts
- Most have eight eyes
- Attacks insects with venom
- May spin webs

Daddy longlegs
- One body part
- All have two eyes
- Does not make venom
- Never spins webs

The daddy longlegs dodges in and out of the leaf litter in search of food. As she moves, her tiny, oval body gently bounces up and down between her long, thin legs. Her body never rises too far above the ground.

Every now and then, the daddy longlegs waves her two longest legs through the air, touching everything within reach. They help her understand the world.

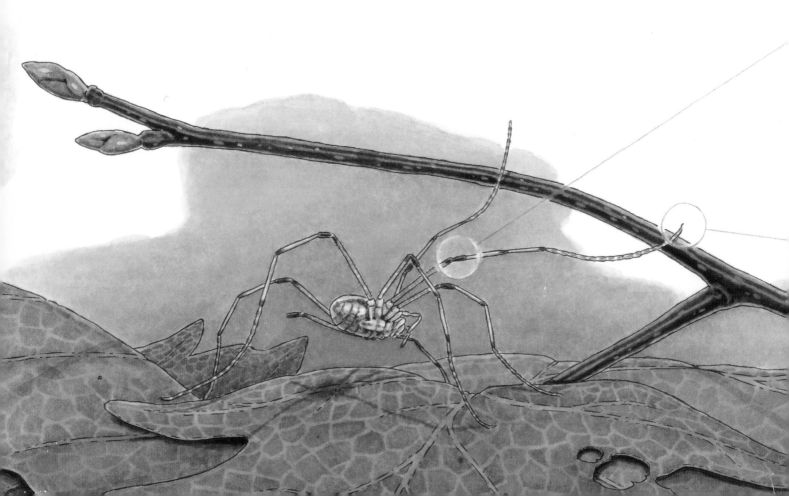

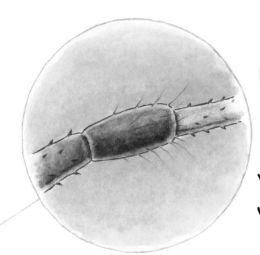

The short, stiff hairs on her longest legs help the daddy longlegs feel.

Very fine hairs at each leg joint sense vibrations traveling through the air. Your ears do the same job.

Sensors at the tip of each leg help the daddy longlegs smell and taste.

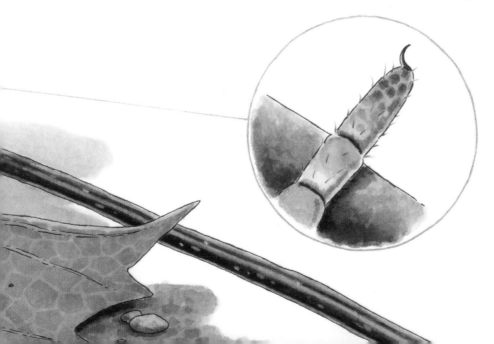

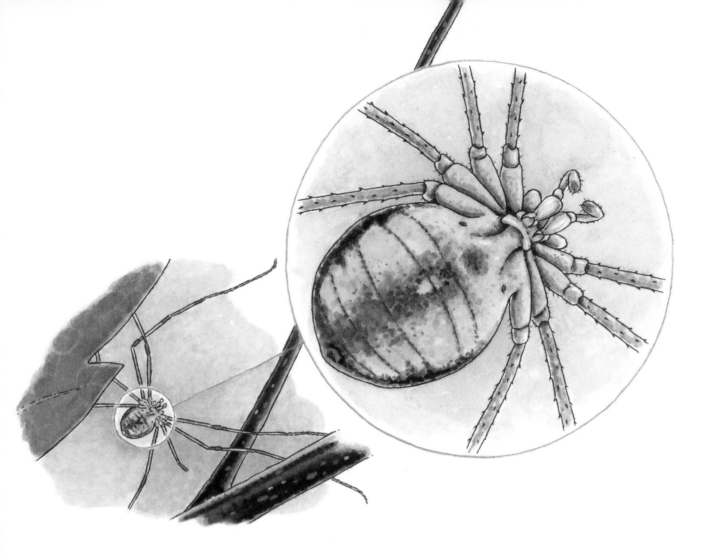

The daddy longlegs takes in air to breathe
through ten small holes in her exoskeleton.
She has one hole near the end of each leg
and two holes behind her rear legs.

When the daddy longlegs feels threatened, a smelly liquid oozes out of two tiny holes behind her front legs. It makes most enemies feel too sick or too weak to devour the daddy longlegs.

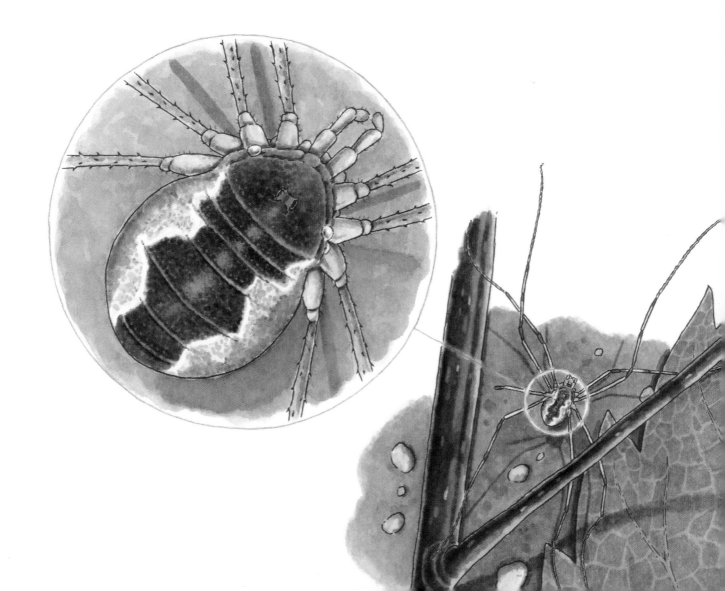

At the edge of the woods, the daddy longlegs finds a pill bug. Two feelers near her slit of a mouth grab the prey and push it into her claw-like pincers. They crush the pill bug and put it into her mouth. She munches on the insect and swallows it down.

As the daddy longlegs explores her surroundings, a hungry American toad sneaks up behind her. It lunges forward, missing her body but catching a leg. The leg wriggles wildly for a few seconds, distracting the toad while the daddy longlegs darts out of sight.

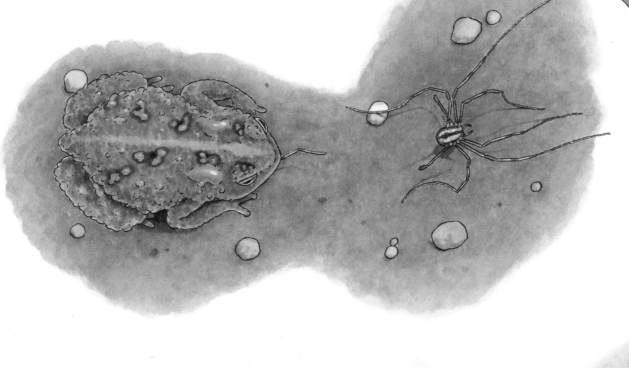

Even with six legs, she can still move quickly.

Now the daddy longlegs is thirsty. She skims gracefully across the top of the grass as she searches for water.

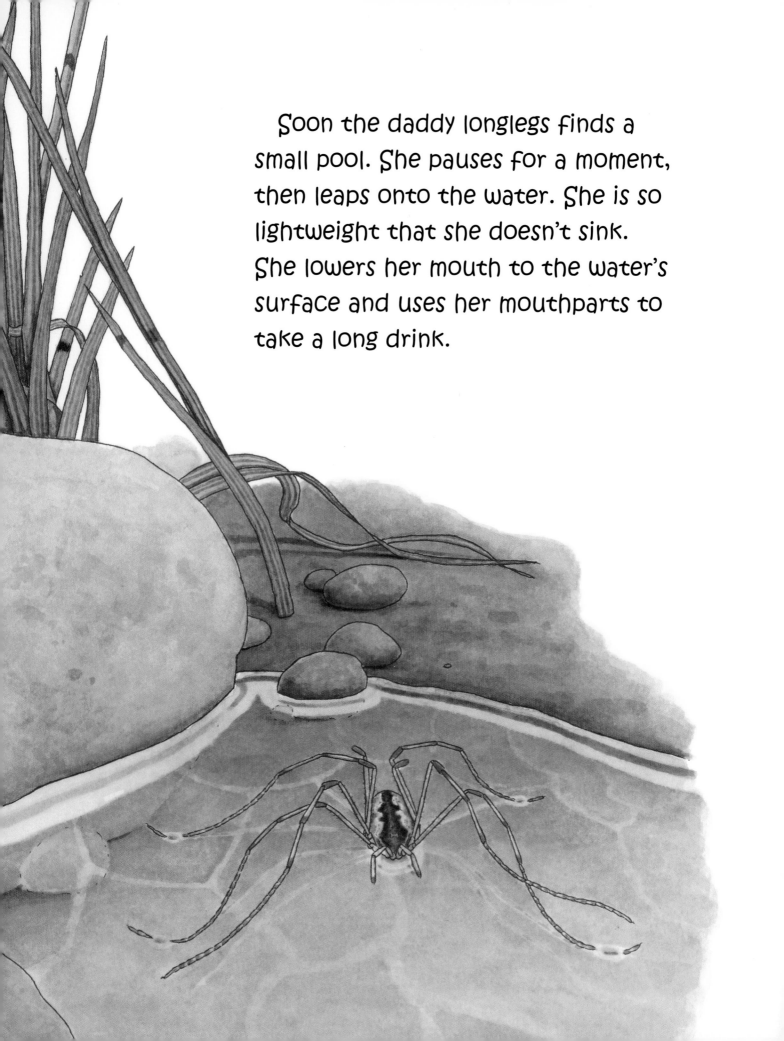

Soon the daddy longlegs finds a small pool. She pauses for a moment, then leaps onto the water. She is so lightweight that she doesn't sink. She lowers her mouth to the water's surface and uses her mouthparts to take a long drink.

Then the daddy longlegs springs toward solid ground, but she falls short. She lands on an autumn leaf that has just blown into the pool. The stream water tugs the leaf this way and that. Soon the daddy longlegs is racing downstream.

But the ride doesn't last long. The leaf and the daddy longlegs crash into a rock. Wearily, she climbs onto land.

After a short rest, the daddy longlegs begins to clean her legs, especially her extra-long ones. Only clean legs can do a good job sensing the world. She slowly pulls each leg through her jaws. When she is done, she carefully rinses her jaws in the stream.

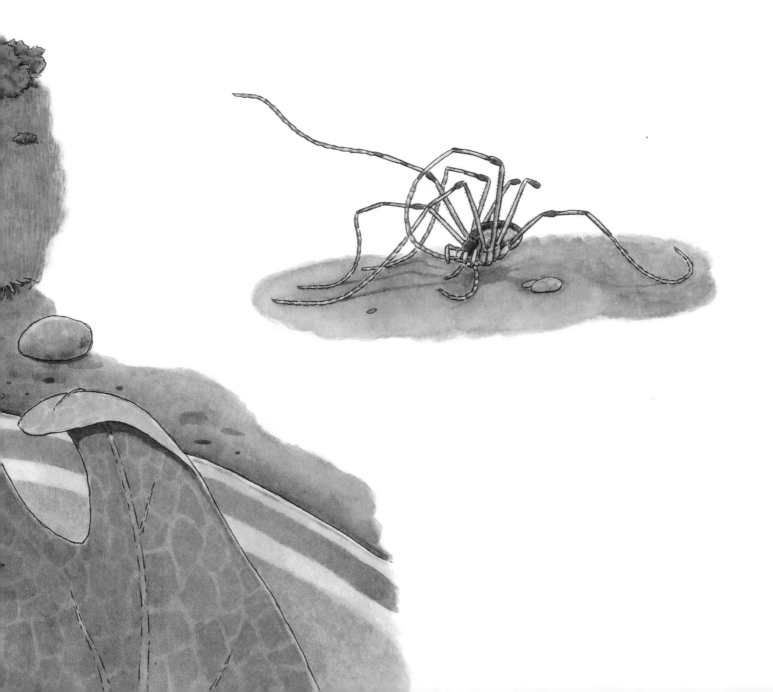

Now the daddy longlegs looks around.
The eyes that stick up above her body
stare sideways. They can't see colors or
understand the shape of objects, but they
can sense light and movement. Right now,
they tell the daddy longlegs it is night.
That means most of her enemies are resting.

She crosses a freshly cut lawn, climbs through some shrubs, and then returns to the ground.

The chilly evening air warns the daddy longlegs that winter is on its way. It is time to find a mate.

As she wanders along the ground, a male daddy longlegs darts out of a rainspout and pounces on her back. The female quickly shakes him off. He scrambles back to her side, and the two daddy longlegs spend a few moments touching one another with their longest legs. The female decides he will make a good mate.

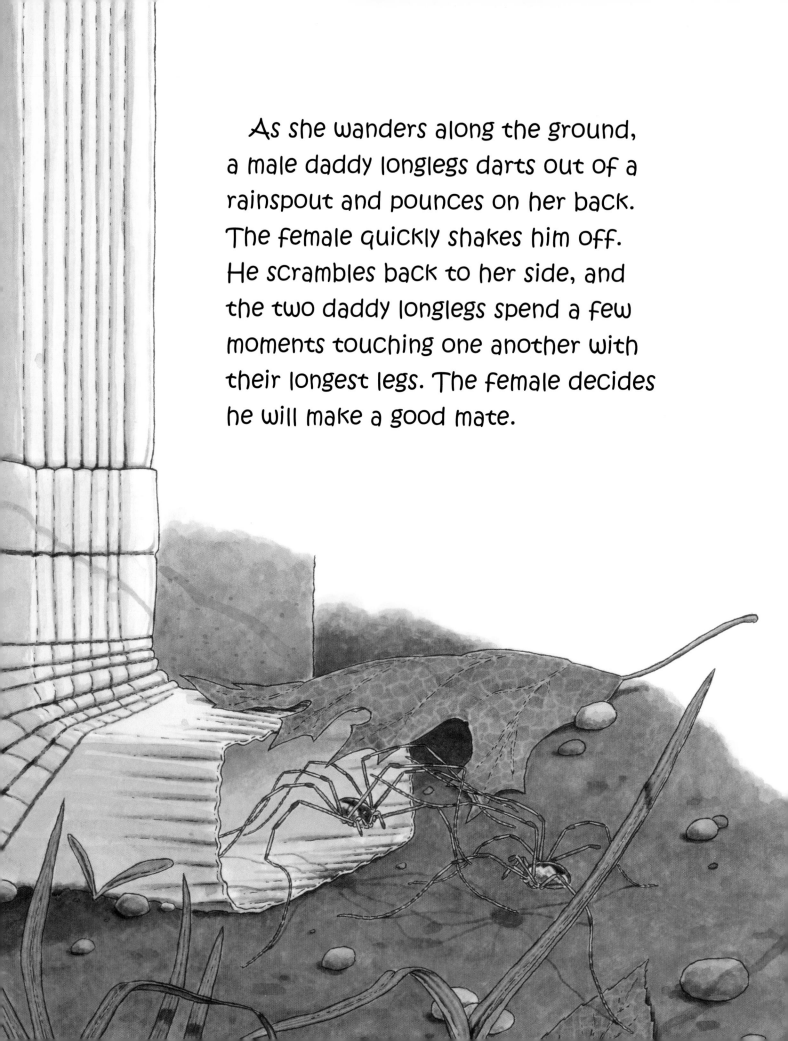

Over the next few days, the daddy longlegs searches for places to hide her eggs. She needs to keep them safe from hungry animals and cold winter weather. The daddy longlegs lays about fifty pale green eggs. She leaves some in the damp soil. She puts others under stones or in shaded crevices.

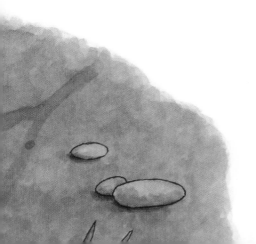

A few weeks later, the daddy longlegs dies.
She cannot survive the long, cold winter.

But in the spring, her eggs
hatch and more daddy longlegs
enter the world.

More About Daddy Longlegs

Not everyone uses the term *daddy longlegs* in the same way. Europeans sometimes use it to describe an insect called the crane fly by people in other parts of the world. In North America, some people call a group of long-legged, web-building spiders *daddy longlegs*. However, the name is most often used to describe a separate group of creatures most commonly seen in the late summer and early autumn. Because this is the time when farmers are harvesting their crops, many scientists use the name *harvestmen* to describe them.

Scientists have identified about 7,000 different kinds of harvestmen on Earth. But there are probably many more left to discover. About 200 kinds of harvestmen live in North America. This book focuses on the striped daddy longlegs, which is common in the eastern half of the United States and Canada.

Throughout most of the striped daddy longlegs' range, adults die in late autumn. In the southern United States, adults may hibernate during the winter and live for several years.

You are most likely to find harvestmen in cool, moist places. Look for them in shaded plant beds, under flowerpots, near rainspouts, and scurrying along shady walls outside buildings or in basements. Although harvestmen sometimes travel short distances in search of food and mates, most stay fairly close to the place they hatched.

If you catch a harvestman, handle it gently and do not keep it for too long. While harvestmen occasionally eat rotting fruit, fungi, or dead insects, most hunt for live prey, especially small insects. Scientists estimate that spiders and harvestmen eat about one half of all the insects that ever hatch.

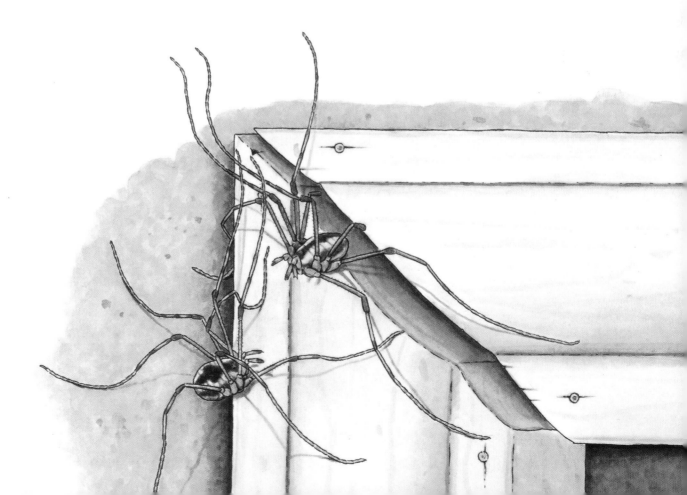

Glossary

aphid—a small wingless insect that sucks plant juices

crevice—a tiny crack or hole

exoskeleton—the hard, protective outer layer that covers the
bodies of insects, spiders, harvestmen, and other animals that
do not have a backbone

fungi—a group of living things that are neither plants nor animals.
This group includes mushrooms, toadstools, yeasts, and many
other tiny creatures.

hibernate—to spend the winter in a resting state. While an animal
hibernates, its heart rate and breathing slow down.

joint—a flexible part that connects non-bending parts

prey—an animal that is hunted, killed, and/or eaten by another animal

venom—a harmful liquid that is injected into prey

vibrations—a pattern of wave-like movements that travel through
the air when a creature moves

To Find Out More

Books

Anderson, Catherine. *Daddy Longlegs*. Chicago, IL:
Heinemann Library, 2008.

Miller, Heather L. *Daddy Longlegs*. San Diego, CA:
KidHaven Press, 2005.

Web Sites

Daddy Longlegs
www.backyardnature.net/longlegs.htm

Daddy Longlegs
www.wnrmag.com/stories/2000/jun00/daddy.htm

The Spider Myths Site
www.washington.edu/burkemuseum/spidermyth/myths/
daddylonglegs.html

About the Author

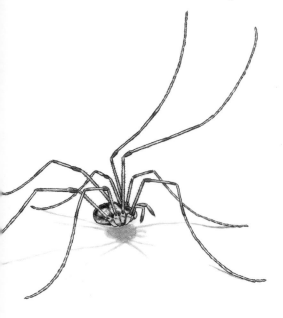

Melissa Stewart is an award-winning author of more than one hundred books for young readers. She has also written articles for such publications as *Ask, Click, Highlights for Children, Odyssey, Ranger Rick, Science World,* and *The Writer.* She serves on the board of advisors for the Society of Children's Book Writers and Illustrators and is a judge for the American Institute of Physics Children's Science Writing Award. Melissa earned a B.S. in biology from Union College and an M.A. in science journalism from New York University. She lives in Acton, Massachusetts, with her husband, Gerard. To learn more about Melissa, please visit www.melissa-stewart.com.

About the Illustrator

John Himmelman is a children's book author, illustrator, and naturalist. He has written and illustrated nearly 70 books, many of them about the wild creatures encountered in North America. He lives with his wife in Killingworth, Connecticut, where he is fortunate to share his backyard with many daddy longlegs! To learn more about John, please visit www.johnhimmelman.com.

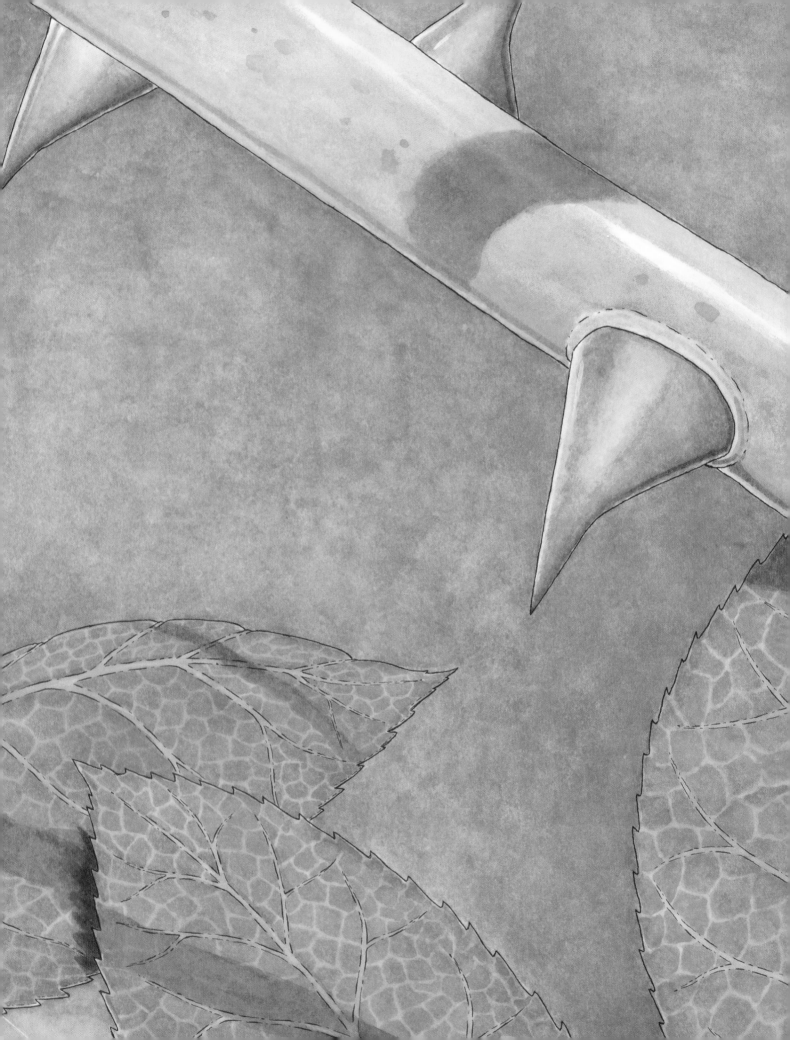